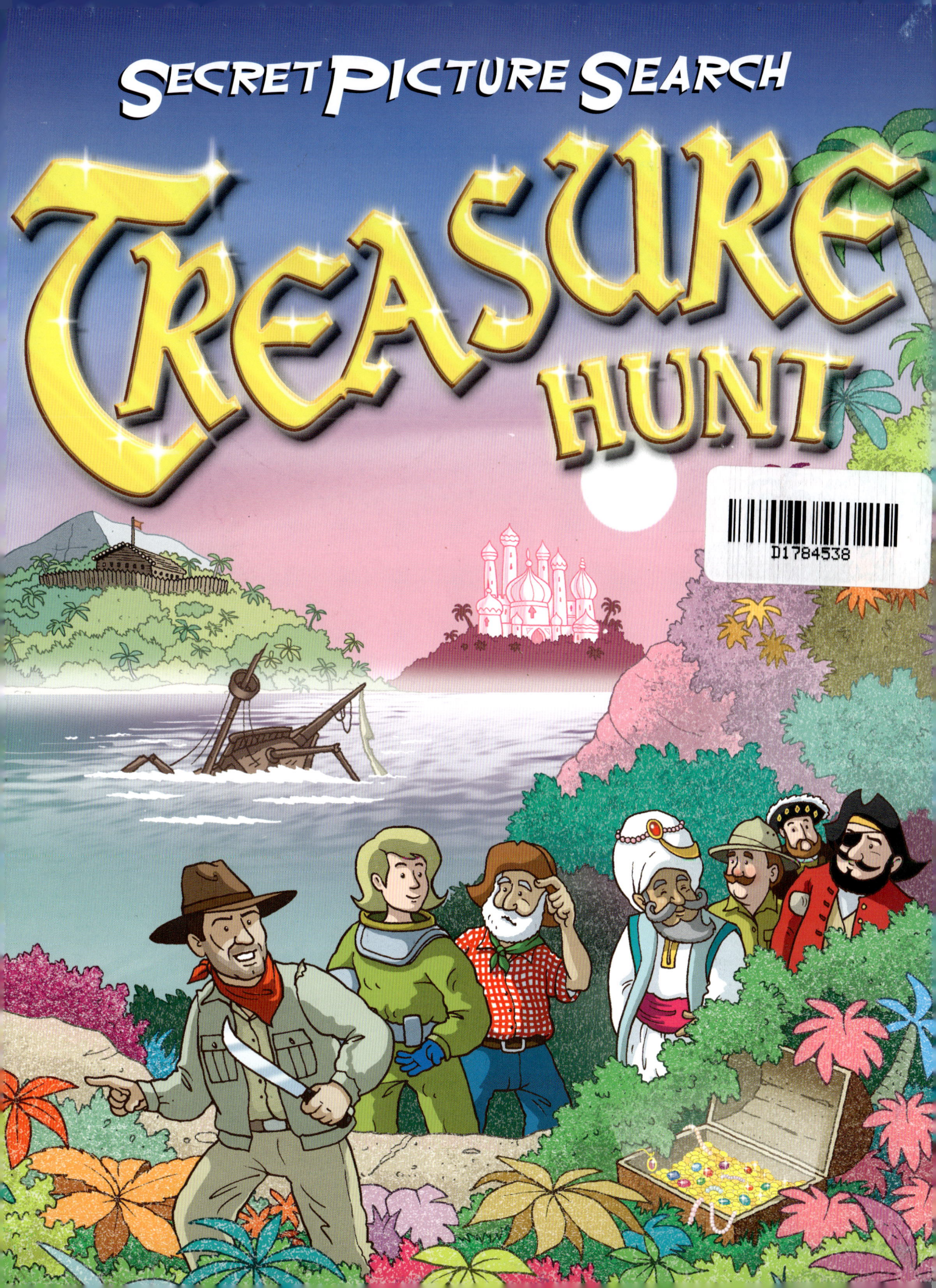

SECRET PICTURE SEARCH

TREASURE HUNT

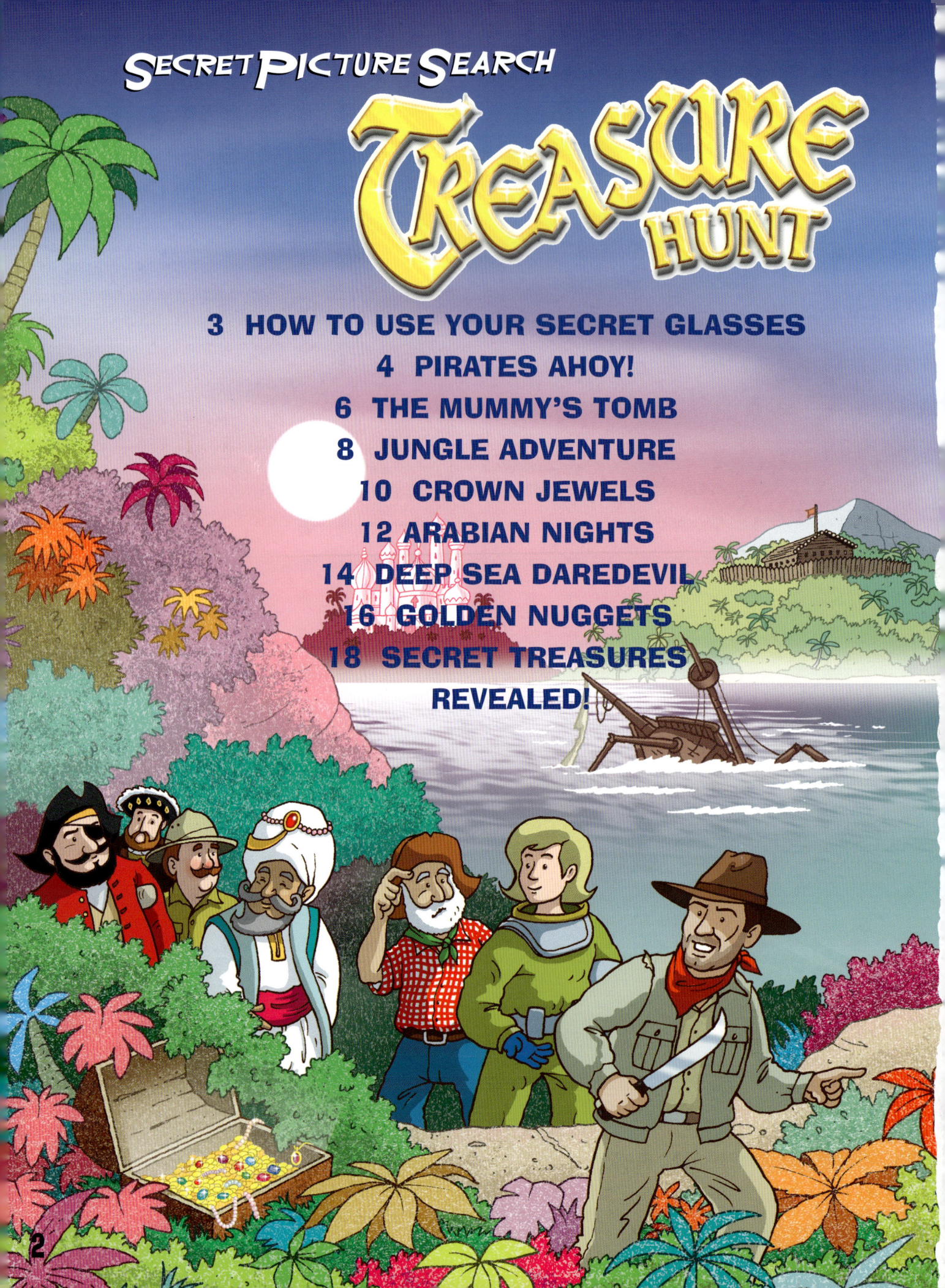

SECRET PICTURE SEARCH

TREASURE HUNT

SECRET GLASSES

HOW TO USE YOUR SECRET GLASSES.

First look at each scene and read the story. There is treasure hidden on every page, with over 100 lost treasures to find.
Put on your Secret Glasses to find and count the secret pictures.
You can check the answers on pages 18 and 19.

Blackeyed Pete, the wicked pirate and terror of the seven seas, may be good at sea battles but he has a terrible memory. He can't remember where he buried his loot! On his secret island

hideaway, he has his pirate crew digging all over the place desperately looking for the treasure. They haven't found it yet. Can you find it first with your secret glasses?

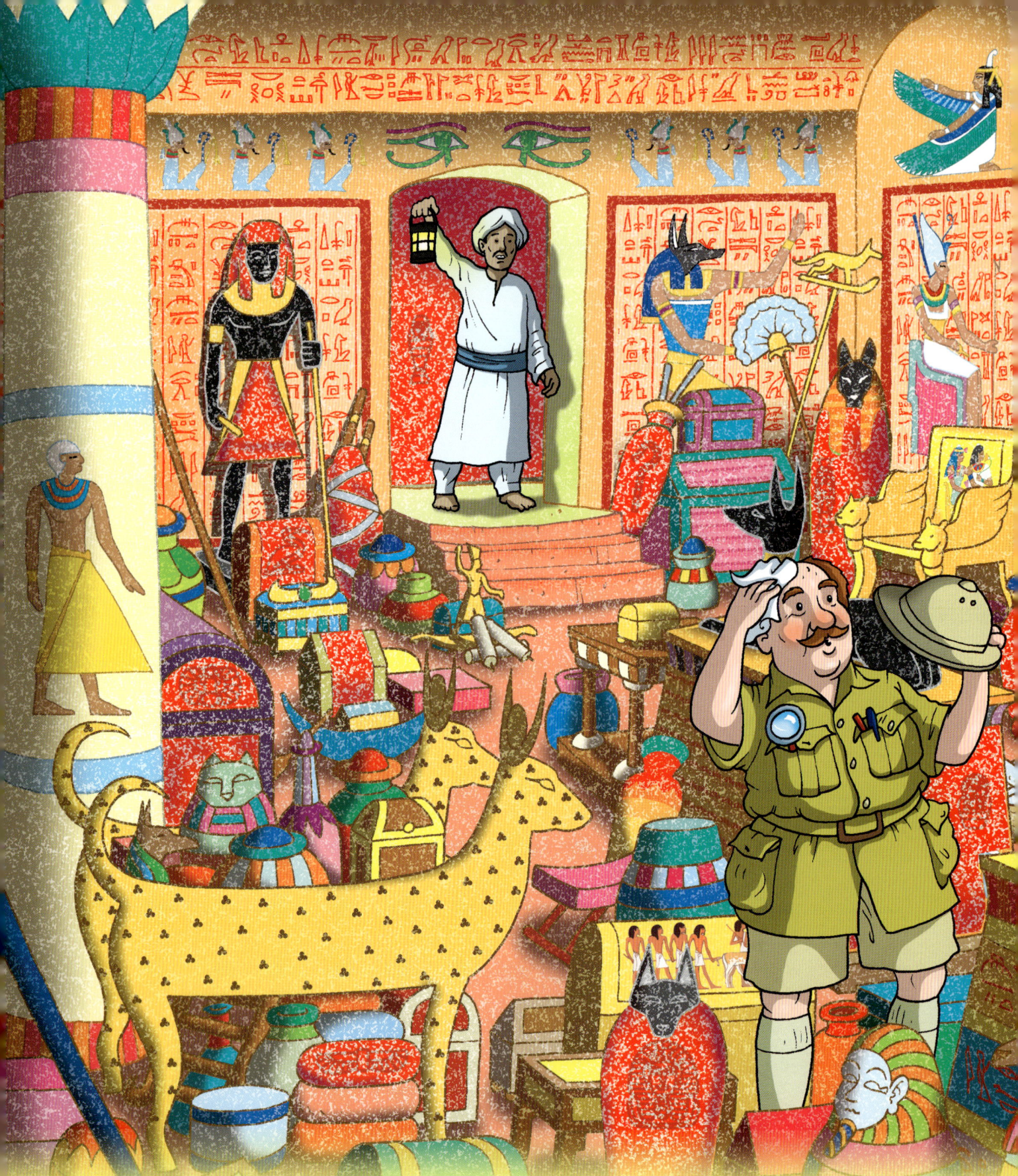

Sir Donald Diggemup, the famous archaeologist, has spent years searching Egypt for the tomb of King Tootancomin. With the help of some local workers, he has stumbled into an old burial

chamber. Could this be King Toot's tomb? Surely there should be gold and jewels - but where are they? Sir Donald is getting hot and bothered. Using your secret glasses, can you help him?

Peruvian Jake is a tough explorer who enjoys risky adventures in search of ancient treasures. Here in South America he is finding it difficult to get through the jungle. He is searching for the

lost city of Muchu Pinchu where hundreds of years ago an ancient civilization built incredible temples and made wonderful treasures from gold and silver. Can you help Jake find them?

Bluff King Hal isn't a cheerful soul this morning – he has woken up to a big shock. The crown jewels have been stolen! Thieves have broken into the castle strongroom and taken the most

fabulous treasures. The guards are running around, searching for the thieves and the stolen jewels. Using your secret glasses maybe you can help find them and put a smile back on the King's face.

Old Sheikh Zandeetoes, a popular ruler in ancient Arabia, is upset – the royal treasure chest is empty! The priceless diamonds that were inside are missing. Where have they gone?

Have they been stolen? The bodyguard is looking very suspicious. Could he have hidden the jewels? The Sheikh will need some special powers to find them – your secret glasses will help.

A long time ago in the Caribbean seas, a Spanish galleon laden with untold riches sank during a mighty storm. In 1955, undersea archaeologist Ursula Wave discovered the wrecked galleon and

searched for the fabulous treasure. Was the treasure still in
the ship? Had raiders been disturbed and dropped some on the
seabed? Use your secret glasses, you might be able to help her.

Poor old Prospector Sam, the Wild West gold miner, has run out of luck. His gold mine is empty and the mineshaft has collapsed. Now Sam must try to find gold nuggets in the river, using his

trusty pan. Will Sam find enough gold to make his fortune? His old friend Wild Willy has come to help. You'd like to help him too, wouldn't you? Put on the secret glasses and find those nuggets!

TREASURE HUNT *SECRETS* REVEALED!

How much hidden treasure did you find? Look on these scrolls to check your answers. Use your Secret Glasses to see the magic total.

4 PIRATES AHOY!

Swashbuckling pirates sailing the seven seas are not a fantasy – many real life pirates took to the seas to plunder merchant ships transporting riches. The skull and crossbones flag of a pirate ship struck terror in the hearts of sailors all around the world.

10 THE CROWN JEWELS

The world famous Crown Jewels of England are kept safe in the Tower of London, one of the world's strongest strongrooms. The Yeomen of the Guard have the important job of making sure they stay there!

12 ARABIAN GEMS

Jewels, like those the Sheikh had lost, take millions of years to form deep underground in rocks – which is one reason they are so valuable. Another is their beauty.

6 MUMMY'S TOMB

Archaeologists are people who like to find out about the way our ancestors lived. They dig into interesting sites and record what they find. Sometimes fantastic priceless treasures are unearthed.

8 JUNGLE ADVENTURE

In the mid 1900s, brave adventurers often went on long trips to far away places in search of their fortunes. The dark jungles of South America and Africa were often favorite destinations for these daring explorers.

14 DEEPSEA DAREDEVIL

Underwater exploration is a dangerous business. Modern divers take an airtank with them when they dive, but not so long ago the only way to explore undersea was to have air pumped down a pipe from a boat.

16 GOLDEN NUGGETS

"There's gold in them there hills!" was the famous saying of the gold prospectors during the North American gold rush of the mid 1800s.

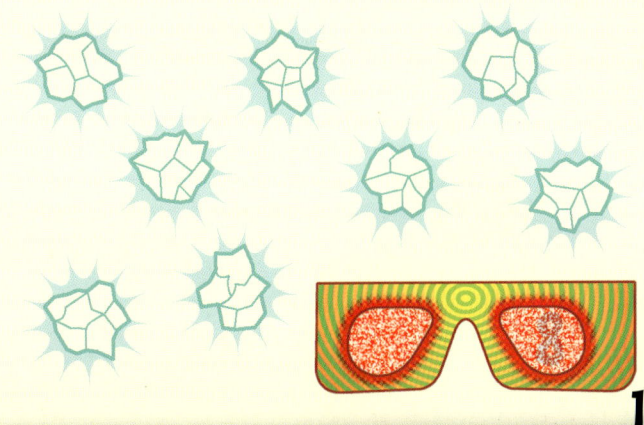